Faith and Healing:

A Therapist's Guide to Spiritual Disorders

APOSTLE: DR. SHAMEKA R CAMPBELL, PhD

CONTEXT

DEDICATION

THIS BOOK IS DEDICATED TO OUR THERAPIST AND COUNSELORS WHO HELP WITH THE MENTAL HEALTH WHETHER DONE CLINICALLY OR SPIRITUALLY. IT WAS WRITTEN TO BRIDGE THE GAP IN THE WAY WE SEE THERAPY, WHETHER FROM A LICENSED STANDPOINT TO A CERTIFIED STANDPOINT. WE ALL COULD COME TOGETHER AND LEARN THE IMPORTANCE OF USING AND IMPLEMENTING BOTH WAYS OF THERAPY AS WHOLESOME HEALING.

Chapter 1: Understanding Spiritual Disorders

Definition and Scope

The concept of spiritual disorders is increasingly recognized within the fields of therapy and counseling, particularly as mental health professionals seek to understand the interplay between spirituality and psychological well-being. Spiritual disorders can be defined as a set of conditions where an individual's spiritual beliefs and practices significantly impact their mental health, leading to symptoms that may mimic or exacerbate traditional mental disorders. This definition emphasizes the importance of considering spiritual dimensions in therapeutic settings, allowing practitioners to adopt a more holistic approach to healing and recovery.

The scope of spiritual disorders encompasses a wide range of experiences, including but not limited to existential crises, spiritual bypassing, and the consequences of religious trauma. These disorders can manifest in various ways, such as anxiety, depression, and feelings of disconnection from self or community. Understanding the nuances of these conditions is crucial for therapists and counselors, as they often require tailored interventions that address both spiritual beliefs and psychological symptoms. Recognizing the specific characteristics of spiritual disorders can enhance the therapeutic alliance and promote more effective healing outcomes.

In the context of the Diagnostic and Statistical Manual of Spiritual Disorders, a framework is proposed for categorizing spiritual issues that may lead to or complicate mental health diagnoses. This manual aims to provide clinicians with a comprehensive guide to identify and understand the intersections between spirituality and mental health. By establishing clear criteria for spiritual disorders, this framework allows practitioners to differentiate between purely psychological issues and those that are deeply rooted in *spiritual distress, thereby improving diagnostic accuracy and treatment planning.*

The importance of this definition and scope extends beyond individual therapy sessions and into community settings, where spiritual leaders and counselors play a pivotal role in addressing the needs of those experiencing spiritual crises. Pastors and ministers, in particular, are often the first point of contact for individuals grappling with spiritual disorders. By equipping these leaders with the knowledge and tools to recognize and respond to spiritual distress, the potential for holistic healing within congregations increases. This collaboration between mental health professionals and spiritual leaders fosters a more integrated approach to care.

Ultimately, understanding the definition and scope of spiritual disorders is essential for promoting comprehensive mental health care. As therapists, counselors, and spiritual leaders work together to support individuals in their healing journeys, they can create a more inclusive model that respects and incorporates the spiritual dimensions of health. This integrative approach not only enhances the effectiveness of therapeutic interventions but also empowers individuals to reclaim their spiritual identities while addressing their mental health needs.

Historical Context

The historical context of faith and healing is deeply intertwined with the evolution of mental health treatment and spiritual beliefs. Throughout history, various cultures have approached mental health through the lens of spirituality, with many ancient civilizations attributing psychological distress to demonic possession, divine punishment, or a disruption in the balance of bodily humors. In these societies, healers, shamans, and priests played crucial roles in addressing both the spiritual and physical ailments of individuals, often employing rituals, prayers, and herbal remedies to restore health. This dual approach laid the groundwork for the later development of more formalized mental health practices.

The rise of organized religion significantly influenced perceptions of mental illness and healing. During the Middle Ages, the Church held considerable power, and mental disorders were often viewed through a moral lens. Individuals exhibiting signs of mental distress were sometimes labeled as sinners or possessed, leading to practices such as exorcisms and severe punishments. This perspective not only stigmatized those suffering from mental disorders but also limited the understanding of mental health to predominantly spiritual interpretations. It was not until the Enlightenment that a more rational and scientific approach began to emerge, paving the way for the eventual separation of spiritual and psychological care.

In the 19th and 20th centuries, the field of psychology began to develop its own identity, moving away from strictly religious interpretations of mental health. The establishment of institutions dedicated to mental health treatment, such as asylums and psychiatric hospitals, marked a shift towards medicalization. However, this period also saw the rise of various spiritual movements that sought to integrate faith with healing. Figures such as Carl Jung explored the connection between spirituality and psychology, suggesting that understanding the psyche requires acknowledging spiritual dimensions. This interplay between faith and psychology introduced new therapeutic modalities, including transpersonal psychology, which emphasizes spiritual experiences and their role in mental health.

The subsequent decades witnessed a growing interest in holistic approaches to healing, leading to the emergence of complementary and alternative therapies. These practices often incorporate spiritual elements, recognizing the importance of addressing the whole person—mind, body, and spirit. Therapists and counselors increasingly began to acknowledge the spiritual aspects of mental health, integrating techniques such as mindfulness, meditation, and prayer into their practices. This recognition of the spiritual dimension in therapy aligns with a broader cultural shift towards valuing individual beliefs and experiences in the healing process.

Today, the intersection of faith and healing continues to evolve, with the recognition that spiritual disorders can significantly impact mental health. The Diagnostic and Statistical Manual of Spiritual Disorders aims to provide a framework for understanding these complex interactions, guiding therapists, counselors, and spiritual leaders in their work with individuals experiencing spiritual distress. By understanding the historical context of faith and healing, professionals can better navigate the challenges presented by spiritual disorders, fostering an environment where both psychological and spiritual needs are addressed in a compassionate and informed manner.

The Intersection of Mental Health and Spirituality

The intersection of mental health and spirituality presents a complex landscape for therapists and counselors, particularly when navigating the nuances of how spiritual beliefs can influence psychological well-being. Mental health professionals often encounter clients whose spiritual experiences are both a source of strength and a potential risk factor for mental disorders. Understanding this interplay is crucial for effective assessment and treatment, especially in the context of the Diagnostic and Statistical Manual of Spiritual Disorders. By exploring the relationship between spirituality and mental health, practitioners can better support clients in their healing journeys.

Spiritual beliefs can serve as protective factors against mental health issues. For many individuals, faith provides a framework for understanding life's challenges, fostering resilience, and promoting coping strategies. Spirituality often encourages community engagement, social support, and a sense of belonging, all of which are critical components of mental wellness. Therapists must recognize the positive aspects of spirituality, incorporating these elements into their therapeutic practices. By validating clients' spiritual beliefs and experiences, practitioners can create a safe space for exploration and healing.

Conversely, spirituality can also contribute to the development or exacerbation of mental health issues. Certain spiritual practices may lead to experiences that resemble psychosis or anxiety disorders, particularly when individuals encounter profound existential questions or crises of faith. The DSM's framework on spiritual disorders highlights how these experiences can manifest in ways that overlap with more traditional mental health diagnoses. It is essential for therapists to differentiate between normative spiritual experiences and those that may indicate a deeper psychological concern, ensuring that clients receive appropriate interventions.

Moreover, integrating spirituality into therapeutic work can enhance treatment outcomes. Techniques such as mindfulness, meditation, and prayer can be beneficial in managing symptoms *of anxiety, depression, and trauma. Therapists should be equipped to incorporate spiritual assessments into their evaluations, exploring clients' beliefs and experiences as part of the therapeutic process. This integration not only validates the client's worldview but also allows for a more holistic approach to treatment that addresses both psychological and spiritual dimensions.*

In conclusion, the intersection of mental health and spirituality calls for a nuanced understanding among therapists, counselors, and spiritual leaders. By recognizing the potential for both healing and harm within spiritual practices, professionals can better navigate the complexities of their clients' experiences. The goal is to foster a therapeutic environment that honors spiritual beliefs while addressing mental health concerns, ultimately guiding individuals toward a path of comprehensive healing. Through collaboration and open dialogue, mental health and spiritual care can coexist, leading to more effective support for those seeking help.

Chapter 2: The Diagnostic Framework

Overview of the DSM and Spiritual Disorders

The Diagnostic and Statistical Manual of Spiritual Disorders (DSSM) serves as a comprehensive framework for understanding how spiritual issues can intersect with mental health problems. In recent years, there has been an increasing recognition of the importance of spirituality in psychological well-being. The DSM categorizes various spiritual disorders that can manifest in ways that affect an individual's mental state. These disorders can stem from crises of faith, spiritual abuse, or even a perceived disconnect from one's spiritual beliefs. Understanding this intersection is crucial for therapists, counselors, pastors, and ministers who aim to provide holistic care that addresses both the mental and spiritual health of their clients.

The DSSM identifies specific categories of spiritual disorders that practitioners should familiarize themselves with. These encompass a range of issues, from existential crises to obsessive spiritual practices. For instance, individuals experiencing a spiritual crisis may exhibit symptoms akin to anxiety or depression, but their root causes may lie in spiritual discontent or unresolved theological questions. By recognizing these patterns, therapists can tailor their interventions to address both the psychological and spiritual dimensions of their clients' distress. This dual approach not only fosters healing but also encourages clients to explore their beliefs and values in a supportive environment.

Additionally, spiritual disorders can often be misdiagnosed as purely psychological issues. This misalignment can lead to ineffective treatment strategies that fail to address the underlying spiritual concerns. Therapists and counselors must cultivate an awareness of how spiritual beliefs and experiences can significantly shape a person's mental health. By integrating spiritual assessments into their practice, professionals can gain insights that enhance their understanding of a client's struggles, ultimately leading to more effective treatment plans. This integration is essential in fostering a therapeutic environment where clients feel safe to discuss their spiritual beliefs and concerns.

The role of spiritual leaders, such as pastors and ministers, is also pivotal in identifying and addressing spiritual disorders. They often serve as the first point of contact for individuals seeking help, making it essential for them to recognize signs of spiritual distress. Training in the principles outlined in the DSSM can empower these leaders to provide appropriate guidance and referrals when necessary. Furthermore, collaboration between mental health professionals and spiritual leaders can create a more comprehensive support system for individuals grappling with spiritual issues, ensuring that both their mental and spiritual needs are met.

In conclusion, the Overview of the DSM and Spiritual Disorders highlights the critical intersection between spirituality and mental health. Awareness of spiritual disorders and their implications can enhance the effectiveness of therapeutic interventions. By acknowledging the role of spirituality in mental health, therapists, counselors, pastors, and ministers can work together to create a more integrated approach to healing. This collaboration not only enriches the therapeutic process but also promotes a more profound understanding of the human experience, ultimately leading to more meaningful and impactful healing journeys for clients.

Criteria for Diagnosis

Criteria for diagnosis in the realm of spiritual disorders necessitate a comprehensive understanding of both psychological and spiritual dimensions. The Diagnostic and Statistical Manual of Spiritual Disorders (DSSDS) serves as a framework for professionals to discern the interplay between faith and mental health. The criteria for diagnosis not only encompass traditional psychological symptoms but also include specific spiritual manifestations that may exacerbate or mimic mental disorders. This dual approach aids therapists, counselors, pastors, and ministers in recognizing the unique challenges faced by individuals experiencing spiritual distress.

One of the primary criteria involves assessing the individual's spiritual beliefs and practices. A thorough evaluation of how these beliefs impact mental health is essential. For instance, an individual may report feelings of despair or confusion that coincide with a crisis of faith or a significant spiritual event. Evaluating the context of these feelings, including the individual's spiritual background, community support, and personal coping mechanisms, provides valuable information for diagnosis. It is crucial that the clinician remains sensitive to the client's spiritual context, as misinterpretation of spiritual experiences can lead to inappropriate diagnoses.

Additionally, it is important to differentiate between normative spiritual experiences and those that indicate a disorder. Certain spiritual phenomena, such as intense mystical experiences or profound feelings of connection, may be misinterpreted as symptoms of a mental health condition. Conversely, symptoms of mental disorders, such as anxiety or depression, might be rooted in spiritual crises. Clinicians must employ careful discernment to determine whether these experiences are a natural part of the individual's spiritual journey or indicative of a deeper issue requiring intervention.

The role of community and support systems also plays a critical part in the diagnostic process. Individuals who experience spiritual disorders often navigate their distress within their faith communities. Evaluating the support and resources available to the individual can provide insight into their coping strategies and overall resilience. A lack of community support may exacerbate feelings of isolation and despair, leading to a more severe presentation of symptoms. Understanding the dynamics of the individual's spiritual environment helps clinicians *formulate a more accurate diagnosis and develop effective treatment plans.*

Finally, the integration of spiritual assessments alongside traditional psychological assessments provides a holistic view of the individual's mental health. Tools such as spiritual history questionnaires, assessments of spiritual coping mechanisms, and reflections on the individual's sense of purpose and meaning in life can enrich the diagnostic process. By embracing a multidimensional approach, therapists, counselors, pastors, and ministers can better understand the intricate relationship between faith and mental health, ensuring that individuals receive the most appropriate care and support for their unique experiences.

Common Misdiagnoses

In the context of spiritual disorders, common misdiagnoses often arise due to the complex interplay between psychological and spiritual symptoms. One prevalent misdiagnosis is the conflation of spiritual crises with anxiety disorders. Individuals experiencing profound existential questions or spiritual distress may present symptoms resembling generalized anxiety or panic attacks. Therapists and counselors must discern whether these symptoms are rooted in psychological conditions or if they stem from a deeper spiritual awakening or crisis. A careful assessment of the individual's spiritual beliefs, practices, and life experiences can aid in distinguishing between these two realms.

Another frequent misdiagnosis involves interpreting spiritual manifestations as symptoms of psychotic disorders. For instance, a person experiencing vivid spiritual visions or auditory experiences may be prematurely diagnosed with schizophrenia. This misdiagnosis can lead to unnecessary medication and stigma, potentially alienating individuals from their spiritual practices. It is crucial for clinicians to investigate the context of these experiences, recognizing that they may hold significant spiritual meaning and not necessarily indicate a pathological condition. A nuanced understanding of the individual's spiritual framework can facilitate a more accurate diagnosis.

Depressive episodes can also be misinterpreted as spiritual despondency. Many individuals in spiritual distress may exhibit signs of depression, such as hopelessness or lack of motivation, which can lead to the assumption that they are suffering from a clinical depressive disorder. However, these feelings may arise from a crisis of faith or a struggle to find meaning in suffering. Therapists should take care to explore the individual's spiritual beliefs and practices, as addressing the spiritual dimensions of their experience may lead to healing and resolution that differs significantly from traditional therapeutic interventions focused solely on mental health.

Additionally, obsessive-compulsive disorder (OCD) is often misdiagnosed in individuals whose compulsions are tied to spiritual or religious practices. Some may engage in repetitive rituals or thoughts that they believe are necessary for spiritual purity or to avoid negative consequences. Mislabeling these behaviors as symptomatic of OCD without understanding their spiritual context can lead to inappropriate treatment approaches. Therapists need to differentiate between genuine

OCD and behaviors that are deeply rooted in an individual's spiritual beliefs, as this distinction can significantly alter the therapeutic strategy employed.

Finally, the intersection of trauma and spiritual disorders can lead to misdiagnoses surrounding post-traumatic stress disorder (PTSD). Clients who have experienced spiritual trauma may exhibit symptoms that resemble those of PTSD, such as hypervigilance or emotional numbing. However, the underlying causes may be intricately tied to their spiritual beliefs and experiences. Acknowledging the spiritual dimension of trauma can enhance therapeutic interventions and promote healing. By recognizing these common misdiagnoses, therapists, counselors, pastors, and ministers can better navigate the complexities of spiritual disorders and provide more effective, compassionate care.

Chapter 3: Types of Spiritual Disorders

Faith-Based Anxiety Disorders

Faith-based anxiety disorders represent a unique intersection between mental health and spirituality, where individuals experience anxiety symptoms that are intertwined with their religious beliefs. These disorders can manifest in various forms, including obsessive thoughts about faith practices, excessive worry about spiritual commitments, or fear of divine judgment. For therapists, counselors, pastors, and ministers, understanding the nuances of these disorders is essential to provide effective support and guidance to those struggling with anxiety that is deeply rooted in their faith.

The Diagnostic and Statistical Manual of Spiritual Disorders (DSSDS) offers a framework for identifying and diagnosing faith-based anxiety disorders. These disorders may not fit neatly into traditional categories of anxiety disorders but can significantly impact an individual's daily functioning and spiritual life. Clinicians should be aware of symptoms such as heightened fear of sin, compulsive prayer or ritual practices, and intrusive thoughts related to faith, which can lead to distress and impairment. By recognizing these specific symptoms, professionals can tailor their therapeutic approaches to address both the mental health and spiritual dimensions of the individual's experience.

Treatment for faith-based anxiety disorders often requires a sensitive and integrative approach. Cognitive Behavioral Therapy (CBT) can be particularly effective, allowing individuals to challenge distorted thoughts about their faith and reduce anxiety. Incorporating spiritual practices, such as prayer and meditation, can also be beneficial when aligned with the individual's beliefs. It is crucial for therapists to maintain an open dialogue about the role of faith in their client's life, ensuring that treatment respects and honors their spiritual values while addressing the psychological aspects of their disorder.

Collaboration between mental health professionals and spiritual leaders can enhance the treatment of faith-based anxiety disorders. Pastors and ministers often possess unique insights into the spiritual struggles of their congregants and can play a pivotal role in providing support and guidance. Establishing a referral system between therapists and spiritual leaders can create a holistic support network for individuals experiencing these disorders. This collaboration can help clients feel understood and supported in both their mental health journey and their spiritual life.

Understanding faith-based anxiety disorders requires a compassionate and informed approach. Therapists, counselors, pastors, and ministers must be equipped with the knowledge to recognize these disorders and the skills to address them effectively. By integrating mental health practices with an understanding of spiritual beliefs, professionals can help individuals navigate their anxiety in a way that fosters healing, resilience, and a deeper connection to their faith. As the dialogue between mental health and spirituality continues to evolve, providing comprehensive care that addresses both dimensions will be essential for promoting overall well-being.

Spiritual Crisis

Spiritual crises can significantly impact an individual's mental health, often manifesting as feelings of disconnection, despair, and confusion regarding one's beliefs and values. These crises may arise from various life experiences, such as loss, trauma, or major life transitions, prompting individuals to question their spiritual beliefs and the meaning of their existence. In the context of therapy and counseling, recognizing and addressing these spiritual crises is essential, as they can exacerbate existing mental health disorders or contribute to the development of new ones. Therapists and counselors must be equipped to identify the signs of a spiritual crisis and understand its implications for the overall well-being of their clients.

A spiritual crisis often presents with symptoms that overlap with those of mental disorders, making accurate diagnosis challenging. Clients may report feelings of emptiness, a sense of alienation, or an inability to find solace in traditional spiritual practices. They might experience anxiety or depression as they grapple with existential questions about their purpose and place in the world. The Diagnostic and Statistical Manual of Spiritual Disorders includes various categories that can help clinicians discern spiritual crises from other mental health issues. Understanding these categories can enable professionals to tailor their therapeutic approaches to meet the unique needs of clients experiencing spiritual turmoil.

Therapists and counselors must employ a compassionate and open-minded approach when working with clients in spiritual crisis. It is crucial to create a safe space where individuals feel comfortable exploring their beliefs and the impact of their crisis on their mental health. Active listening, empathy, and validation of the client's experiences can foster a therapeutic alliance that encourages exploration and healing. Additionally, integrating spiritual assessment tools into therapy can help clinicians gauge the severity of the crisis and guide appropriate interventions that align with the client's spiritual beliefs.

Interventions for a spiritual crisis can vary widely, ranging from traditional psychotherapy techniques to more spiritually-oriented practices. Cognitive-behavioral therapy may assist clients in reframing negative thought patterns associated with their crisis, while mindfulness and meditation can provide tools to cultivate inner peace and resilience. Additionally, incorporating spiritual practices such as prayer, ritual, or community engagement can help clients reconnect with their spiritual roots and foster a sense of belonging. It is vital for therapists to remain adaptable and respectful of each client's unique spiritual journey, ensuring that interventions resonate with their beliefs and values.

Finally, the role of faith leaders, such as pastors and ministers, is crucial in addressing spiritual crises within their communities. They can serve as supportive figures who provide guidance and comfort during challenging times, helping individuals navigate their spiritual struggles. Collaboration between mental health professionals and faith leaders can enhance the support available to those experiencing spiritual crises, creating a holistic approach to healing that encompasses both psychological and spiritual dimensions. Through this collaboration, therapists and spiritual leaders can work together to recognize and address the intricate relationships between spirituality and mental health, ultimately promoting a more comprehensive understanding of healing.

Religious Obsessions and Compulsions

Religious obsessions and compulsions represent a unique intersection of spirituality and mental health, often complicating the therapeutic landscape for individuals seeking both religious fulfillment and psychological stability. These disorders manifest as intrusive thoughts or compulsive behaviors that are tied to religious beliefs, leading individuals to experience significant distress. The Diagnostic and Statistical Manual of Mental Disorders (DSM) recognizes such manifestations, yet they often require additional sensitivity when understood through the lens of faith. For therapists, counselors, and spiritual leaders, the challenge lies in distinguishing between genuine spiritual experiences and those that are symptomatic of a mental health disorder.

Individuals experiencing religious obsessions may find themselves plagued by persistent fears or doubts about their faith. This can include excessive worry about sinning, doubts regarding divine acceptance, or fears of eternal damnation. These intrusive thoughts can lead to a cycle of anxiety, causing the individual to engage in compulsive behaviors aimed at alleviating their distress. For example, they may feel compelled to pray excessively, seek constant reassurance from spiritual leaders, or engage in ritualistic behaviors that they believe will protect them from perceived spiritual threats. Understanding the underlying psychological mechanisms can help therapists develop effective treatment plans tailored to the individual's specific beliefs and experiences.

Compulsive religious behaviors often serve as coping mechanisms but can ultimately exacerbate the individual's distress. These behaviors may include repetitive prayer, ritualistic reading of sacred texts, or extreme adherence to religious doctrines. While these actions may initially provide comfort, they can lead to social isolation, hinder daily functioning, and create a barrier to genuine spiritual experiences. It is crucial for mental health professionals to approach these behaviors with empathy, recognizing their potential roots in anxiety or obsessive-compulsive disorder (OCD), rather than dismissing them as mere fanaticism.

Therapists and spiritual leaders must also navigate the ethical considerations involved in treating religious obsessions and compulsions. It is vital to respect the individual's faith while also addressing the mental health aspects of their experience. This balance requires a nuanced understanding of the individual's belief system and an open dialogue about the impact of their compulsions on their overall well-being. Collaborative approaches that include both psychological strategies and spiritual support can foster healing, enabling individuals to find a healthier relationship with their faith.

In conclusion, recognizing and addressing religious obsessions and compulsions is essential for effective therapy in individuals struggling with faith-related mental health issues. By fostering an environment of understanding and respect, therapists, counselors, and spiritual leaders can help individuals navigate the complexities of their spiritual experiences. This integrative approach not only aids in alleviating distress but also encourages a more profound and authentic connection to their faith, paving the way for holistic healing and personal growth.

Chapter 4: Assessment Techniques

Interviewing for Spiritual Issues

Interviewing for spiritual issues requires a nuanced approach, as these matters often intertwine with a client's mental health. The therapist must create a safe and welcoming environment where clients feel comfortable discussing their spiritual beliefs and experiences. This initial rapport is crucial in enabling clients to open up about their spiritual struggles, whether they relate to a crisis of faith, existential questions, or feelings of disconnection from their spiritual community. Building trust allows the therapist to gather more accurate and comprehensive information about the client's spiritual life and its impact on their mental well-being.

During the interview process, it is essential to use open-ended questions that encourage clients to elaborate on their spiritual beliefs and experiences. Questions such as, "Can you describe your understanding of spirituality?" or "How do your spiritual beliefs influence your daily life?" can provide valuable insights. Therapists should also consider exploring any spiritual practices the client engages in, such as prayer, meditation, or participation in religious rituals. Understanding these practices can help identify how they may either contribute to or alleviate the client's mental health issues, providing a clearer picture of the interplay between spirituality and psychological well-being.

It is important to remain sensitive to the diverse spiritual beliefs that clients may hold. Some clients may adhere to organized religions, while others may have a more personal or eclectic spirituality. Therapists should be mindful of their own biases and avoid imposing their beliefs on clients. Demonstrating cultural competence in spiritual matters enhances the therapeutic alliance and encourages clients to share their experiences without fear of judgment. This respectful exploration of spiritual issues can uncover underlying spiritual disorders that may be contributing to the client's mental health challenges.

Therapists should also be aware of the signs of spiritual distress, which may manifest as feelings of hopelessness, disconnection, or a loss of meaning. These symptoms can indicate deeper issues that require careful exploration. Inquiring about significant life events, such as loss, trauma, or transitions in faith, can help identify potential triggers for spiritual crises. By addressing these issues, therapists can assist clients in finding meaning and reconnecting with their spirituality, which may be crucial for their healing journey.

Lastly, it is vital to integrate the insights gained from the interview into the therapeutic process. This may involve collaborating with the client to develop strategies that incorporate their spiritual beliefs into their healing. Whether through mindfulness practices, involvement in community religious activities, or the exploration of philosophical questions, the therapeutic approach should honor the client's spiritual identity. By recognizing and addressing spiritual issues in therapy, practitioners can facilitate a holistic healing process that acknowledges the profound connection between faith and mental health.

Diagnostic Tools and Surveys

Diagnostic tools and surveys play a crucial role in identifying spiritual disorders that may contribute to mental health issues. For therapists, counselors, pastors, and ministers, understanding these tools is essential in providing a holistic approach to treatment. One widely recognized framework is the Diagnostic and Statistical Manual of Spiritual Disorders (DSSDS). This manual categorizes various spiritual disorders that can manifest in ways similar to mental health issues, enabling professionals to better understand their clients' struggles. By integrating spiritual assessments with traditional mental health evaluations, practitioners can create more comprehensive treatment plans.

Surveys designed specifically for assessing spiritual well-being and distress are invaluable resources for professionals working within faith-based contexts. These surveys often include questions on personal beliefs, spiritual practices, and experiences with faith crises. By employing these instruments, therapists can gauge the influence of spirituality on their clients' mental health. The results can reveal underlying spiritual conflicts that may exacerbate psychological symptoms, leading to more targeted interventions. Additionally, surveys can help clinicians monitor changes over time, thereby assessing the effectiveness of therapeutic approaches that incorporate spiritual dimensions.

One important aspect of using diagnostic tools and surveys is ensuring cultural sensitivity and awareness of diverse spiritual beliefs. Different faith traditions may have unique expressions of spirituality, which can affect how individuals experience and report their spiritual struggles. For instance, a survey designed for a Christian audience may not resonate with individuals from other faith backgrounds. Therefore, it is essential for practitioners to adapt tools as needed, ensuring questions are inclusive and relevant to the spiritual beliefs of their clients. This cultural competence not only fosters trust but also enhances the accuracy of the assessments.

In addition to surveys, interviews and case studies can provide deeper insights into the spiritual lives of clients. Open-ended questions allow individuals to share their narratives, highlighting how their spiritual experiences intersect with their mental health challenges. This qualitative data can enrich the understanding of spiritual disorders, moving beyond standardized measures to capture the complexities of individual experiences. By combining quantitative and qualitative methods, professionals can develop a more nuanced understanding of how spiritual issues manifest in their clients' lives.

Ultimately, the integration of diagnostic tools and surveys in the assessment of spiritual disorders represents a significant advancement in therapeutic practice. By recognizing the interplay between spirituality and mental health, therapists and counselors can offer more effective support to those grappling *with spiritual distress. As the field continues to evolve, ongoing research and development of these tools will be vital in enhancing the ability of practitioners to address the unique needs of their clients. This comprehensive approach not only aids in diagnosis but also fosters healing, promoting overall well-being through the integration of spiritual care in therapeutic settings.*

Incorporating Spirituality into Therapy

Incorporating spirituality into therapy involves understanding the profound impact that spiritual beliefs and practices can have on an individual's mental health. Therapists, counselors, and ministers must recognize that spirituality can be a significant source of strength and resilience for many clients. Integrating spiritual principles into therapeutic interventions can foster a holistic approach that addresses not just the psychological symptoms but also the spiritual needs of the individual. This integration requires an open-minded perspective, as well as a willingness to explore the spiritual dimensions of a client's life within the context of their mental health struggles.

Therapists should begin by assessing the spiritual beliefs and practices of their clients during the initial sessions. This assessment can be done through open-ended questions that encourage clients to discuss their spiritual experiences and the role spirituality plays in their daily lives. Understanding a client's spiritual background helps therapists to tailor their interventions more effectively. For instance, if a client derives comfort from prayer or meditation, incorporating these practices into the therapeutic process can enhance their coping mechanisms and promote a sense of peace. Additionally, being aware of spiritual struggles can help therapists identify potential areas of conflict that may exacerbate mental health issues.

The DSM of Spiritual Disorders offers a framework for identifying specific spiritual issues that may contribute to mental health challenges. By recognizing disorders such as spiritual trauma, religious obsession, or existential anxiety, therapists can develop targeted strategies that address both the psychological and spiritual dimensions of a client's experience. This dual approach can facilitate healing by allowing clients to explore their beliefs, confront spiritual crises, and ultimately find meaning in their suffering. It is crucial for therapists to remain sensitive to the diverse spiritual landscapes of their clients, avoiding assumptions that may hinder therapeutic progress.

Incorporating spirituality into therapy also involves creating a safe and supportive environment where clients feel free to express their spiritual concerns. This can be achieved by using affirming language and demonstrating openness to discussing spiritual matters. Therapists can encourage clients to explore their values, beliefs, and practices, fostering a dialogue that validates their experiences. Incorporating spiritual rituals or exercises, such as guided imagery or reflective journaling, can further enhance this exploration. The therapeutic alliance can deepen when clients perceive their therapist as a compassionate ally in their spiritual journey.

Ultimately, the integration of spirituality into therapy is not about imposing specific beliefs but rather about recognizing and honoring the spiritual dimensions of a client's life. By doing so, therapists can provide a more comprehensive form of care *that acknowledges the interconnectedness of mind, body, and spirit. This approach not only enriches the therapeutic process but also empowers clients to engage in their healing journey with a greater sense of purpose and hope. As therapists embrace this holistic perspective, they can contribute to the development of a more inclusive and compassionate framework for mental health care that respects and incorporates the spiritual lives of those they serve.*

Chapter 5: Treatment Modalities

Integrative Therapies

Integrative therapies encompass a wide range of practices that combine traditional therapeutic approaches with complementary and alternative methods. This subchapter explores the significance of integrative therapies in addressing spiritual disorders, which, as noted in the Diagnostic and Statistical Manual of Spiritual Disorders, can manifest as mental health issues. By understanding and incorporating these therapies into practice, therapists, counselors, pastors, and ministers can offer a more holistic approach to healing that encompasses the mind, body, and spirit.

One of the foundational aspects of integrative therapies is the recognition of the interconnectedness of mental, emotional, and spiritual well-being. Many spiritual disorders, such as existential crises or spiritual bypassing, can lead to significant psychological distress. Integrative therapies allow practitioners to address these concerns from multiple angles, employing techniques such as mindfulness, meditation, and breathwork alongside conventional therapeutic methods. By fostering a safe and supportive environment, therapists can guide clients through their spiritual challenges while also addressing their mental health needs.

Incorporating integrative therapies requires an understanding of the diverse modalities available. These can range from art and music therapy to energy healing practices such as Reiki or acupuncture. For clients experiencing spiritual struggles, these alternative therapies can provide unique avenues for expression and healing that traditional talk therapy may not fully address. By incorporating these modalities, practitioners can help clients explore their spirituality in a way that resonates with them personally, encouraging deeper introspection and healing.

The role of community and support systems also plays a critical part in integrative therapies. Group therapy, support groups, and spiritual communities can enhance the healing process for individuals grappling with spiritual disorders. These settings provide an opportunity for shared experiences and mutual support, which can be particularly beneficial when dealing with issues like grief, loss, or crisis of faith. Encouraging clients to engage in community activities or spiritual practices can help them feel less isolated and more connected to their spiritual journey.

Finally, it is essential for therapists, counselors, pastors, and ministers to remain open to ongoing education and training in integrative therapies. As the field of mental health continues to evolve, new research and practices emerge that can enhance the understanding and treatment of spiritual disorders. By staying informed about these developments, practitioners can better serve their clients and foster a more comprehensive approach to healing that honors both their mental health and spiritual needs. Integrative therapies not only support recovery but also empower clients to embrace their spirituality as a vital component of their overall health.

Cognitive-Behavioral Approaches

Cognitive-behavioral approaches (CBT) have gained prominence in therapeutic settings for addressing a wide range of mental health issues, including those intertwined with spiritual disorders. These methods focus on the interplay between thoughts, feelings, and behaviors, making them particularly effective in addressing the cognitive distortions that may arise from spiritual crises or conflicts. By helping clients identify and challenge negative thought patterns, therapists can facilitate a process of healing that integrates both psychological and spiritual dimensions.

At the core of cognitive-behavioral therapy is the understanding that our thoughts significantly influence our emotions and behaviors. When individuals experience spiritual distress, their cognitive frameworks may become skewed, leading to feelings of guilt, anxiety, or despair. Therapists can utilize CBT techniques to assist clients in recognizing these distortions, such as catastrophizing or personalization, which often exacerbate their mental health struggles. By reframing these thoughts, clients may find relief not only from their emotional pain but also from the spiritual turmoil they experience.

A key component of CBT is the use of behavioral interventions that encourage clients to engage in activities aligned with their values and beliefs. This is particularly relevant for those dealing with spiritual disorders, as reconnecting with one's faith or spiritual practices can be a powerful catalyst for healing. Therapists can guide clients in developing exposure exercises that gradually reintroduce them to spiritual environments or practices that they may have withdrawn from due to their mental health challenges. This gradual approach allows clients to confront fears and anxieties in a supportive context, fostering resilience and a renewed sense of purpose.

Incorporating spiritual components into CBT can further enhance its effectiveness. Therapists can work collaboratively with clients to integrate their spiritual beliefs into the cognitive restructuring process. For example, if a client holds beliefs about divine punishment, therapists can help them explore these beliefs in light of a more compassionate understanding of spirituality. This can involve discussions about grace, forgiveness, and the nature of a higher power, promoting a healthier and more supportive framework for the client's emotional and spiritual well-being.

Finally, the application of cognitive-behavioral approaches in the context of spiritual disorders underscores the importance of a holistic therapeutic strategy. By addressing both cognitive distortions and spiritual beliefs, therapists, counselors, and ministers can provide comprehensive support to clients. This integrative approach not only aids in alleviating mental health symptoms but also fosters a deeper connection to one's faith, promoting overall healing and well-being. As professionals dedicated to guiding individuals through their spiritual and psychological challenges, understanding and implementing CBT can be a transformative tool in the therapeutic process.

Spiritual Counseling Techniques

Spiritual counseling techniques encompass a variety of approaches that integrate psychological principles with spiritual beliefs, allowing therapists and counselors to address the unique needs of clients experiencing spiritual disorders. These techniques are grounded in the understanding that spiritual well-being is essential for overall mental health. By recognizing the interplay between spirituality and psychological distress, professionals can create therapeutic environments that promote healing through faith and spiritual exploration.

One effective technique is the use of active listening and empathy. Therapists should create a safe space where clients feel valued and understood. By actively listening to clients' spiritual experiences and concerns, therapists can validate their feelings and help them articulate their beliefs. This process fosters a deeper connection and enables clients to explore their spiritual struggles openly. Empathetic responses can facilitate healing by acknowledging the importance of faith in the client's life and its impact on their mental well-being.

Another vital technique is the incorporation of mindfulness and meditation practices. Mindfulness allows clients to cultivate awareness of their thoughts and feelings in the present moment, promoting a sense of peace and grounding. Integrating spiritual elements into mindfulness practices, such as focusing on a divine presence or reciting spiritual affirmations, can enhance their effectiveness. By teaching clients to engage in these practices, therapists can help them develop coping strategies that align with their spiritual beliefs, ultimately leading to reduced anxiety and improved emotional resilience.

Exploring religious texts and spiritual literature can also serve as a powerful counseling technique. By guiding clients through passages that resonate with their experiences, therapists can facilitate discussions that promote insight and reflection. This technique allows clients to find meaning and solace in their faith, reinforcing their spiritual identity. It also provides a framework for clients to articulate their struggles and aspirations, making it easier for therapists to identify underlying spiritual disorders and tailor interventions accordingly.

Finally, group therapy or support groups centered around spiritual themes can be an effective technique for fostering community and shared healing experiences. These settings allow individuals to connect with others facing similar challenges, creating a sense of belonging and mutual support. Group discussions can facilitate the sharing of personal narratives, spiritual practices, and coping strategies, enriching the healing process. By emphasizing the communal aspects of spirituality, therapists can help clients find strength in their faith and develop a supportive network that encourages ongoing spiritual growth.

Chapter 6: Case Studies

Case Study: Faith-Based Anxiety

The intersection of faith and mental health can present unique challenges, particularly in cases of anxiety influenced by spiritual beliefs. This case study examines an individual, referred to as Sarah, whose experiences illustrate the complexities of faith-based anxiety. Sarah, a 32-year-old woman with a deep commitment to her religious community, sought therapy after experiencing debilitating anxiety that she attributed to her spiritual practices. Her case provides insight into how spirituality can both exacerbate and alleviate anxiety symptoms, offering valuable lessons for therapists and counselors working within faith contexts.

Sarah's anxiety manifested primarily around her interpretation of religious texts and teachings. She often felt an overwhelming pressure to adhere to the moral and ethical standards set forth by her faith, leading to intrusive thoughts and obsessive behaviors aimed at ensuring her compliance. This created a cycle of fear and guilt, where any perceived failure to meet these standards intensified her anxiety. Her case highlights the importance of understanding how specific spiritual beliefs can contribute to the development of anxiety disorders, as they may lead individuals to engage in compulsive behaviors as a means of seeking reassurance or avoiding perceived spiritual consequences.

During therapy, it became essential to help Sarah differentiate between her spiritual beliefs and her mental health symptoms. Cognitive-behavioral techniques were employed to address her intrusive thoughts, while simultaneously validating her faith.

For instance, reframing her understanding of divine expectations helped reduce feelings of inadequacy. Through this process, Sarah began to see that her faith could coexist with her humanity, allowing her to embrace imperfection without the weight of guilt. This dual approach underscores the need for therapists to be culturally competent and sensitive to the spiritual dimensions of a client's experience.

In exploring the roots of Sarah's anxiety, it became evident that her community played a significant role in shaping her beliefs. The pressure to conform to the ideals of her faith community amplified her anxiety, as she feared judgment and ostracism. This case illustrates the potential for community dynamics to influence mental health, making it crucial for therapists to consider the broader context of a client's spiritual life. Facilitating open discussions about these community pressures can empower clients to navigate their spirituality in a healthier way, fostering resilience and self-acceptance.

Ultimately, Sarah's journey towards healing involved integrating her faith with therapeutic practices. By establishing a supportive environment that respected her spiritual beliefs while addressing her mental health needs, she was able to develop coping mechanisms that honored both aspects of her identity. This case study serves as a reminder of the intricate relationship between faith and mental health, emphasizing the necessity for therapists, counselors, and spiritual leaders to engage collaboratively in supporting individuals facing faith-based anxiety. Understanding and addressing these complexities can lead to more effective interventions and promote holistic well-being.

Case Study: Spiritual Crisis

In the context of spiritual disorders, a spiritual crisis can manifest in various ways, often presenting challenges that intertwine psychological distress with spiritual dilemmas. This case study illustrates the experience of a client named Sarah, a 32-year-old woman who sought therapy after experiencing a profound disconnection from her faith. Sarah had been an active member of her church, participating regularly in community activities and prayer groups. However, following a traumatic event in her life—specifically, the sudden death of a close family member—she found herself questioning the very foundations of her beliefs, leading to feelings of isolation and despair.

During the initial assessment, it became evident that Sarah was grappling with symptoms that aligned with both anxiety and depression, as highlighted in the Diagnostic and Statistical Manual of Mental Disorders (DSM). She reported persistent feelings of emptiness, a loss of purpose, and difficulty finding meaning in her life. Furthermore, Sarah experienced intrusive thoughts that challenged her previous convictions about faith and spirituality. In therapy, it became crucial to differentiate between her psychological symptoms and her spiritual crisis, as both elements contributed to her overall mental health.

As therapy progressed, it was essential to explore Sarah's spiritual beliefs and how they had been affected by her trauma. This exploration involved discussing her understanding of God, the afterlife, and the role of faith in coping with loss. Through guided conversations, Sarah began to articulate her feelings of abandonment and anger towards the divine, emotions that had surfaced in the wake of her family member's death. This process not only facilitated a deeper understanding of her spiritual crisis but also helped in identifying the cognitive distortions that fueled her distress.

Interventions focused on integrating spiritual care into the therapeutic process proved beneficial for Sarah. Mindfulness practices and spiritual reflection exercises were introduced to help her reconnect with her faith in a manner that felt authentic and safe. These interventions allowed her to explore her grief while also considering new frameworks of understanding her spirituality. The therapy sessions became a space for Sarah to navigate her questions and doubts without judgment, fostering an environment conducive to healing.

Ultimately, Sarah's journey through her spiritual crisis highlights the intricate relationship between mental health and spirituality. By addressing both aspects in therapy, she was able to find a renewed sense of purpose and redefine her beliefs in a way that honored her experiences. This case study underscores the importance of therapists, counselors, and spiritual leaders recognizing the signs of spiritual distress, as it can significantly impact an individual's mental health and overall well-being. In doing so, they can adopt a holistic approach that not only addresses psychological symptoms but also supports clients in their spiritual journeys.

Case Study: Religious Obsessions

Religious obsessions are a significant area of concern within the context of spiritual disorders, warranting careful consideration by therapists, counselors, and religious leaders. These obsessions are characterized by intrusive thoughts or compulsive behaviors that revolve around religious themes, often leading to considerable distress and impairment in daily functioning. Individuals may experience persistent doubts about their faith, fears of divine punishment, or an overwhelming need to perform religious rituals repeatedly. Such obsessions can mirror the symptoms of obsessive-compulsive disorder, yet they are distinct in their focus on spiritual beliefs and practices.

In the diagnostic framework, it is essential to differentiate between normative religious experiences and pathological religious obsessions. While many individuals engage in spiritual practices that enhance their well-being, those with religious obsessions may find themselves trapped in a cycle of anxiety and compulsivity. For example, a person might repeatedly pray for forgiveness, fearing that they have committed unforgivable sins, even when rational evidence suggests otherwise. This form of obsessive behavior can lead to significant disruptions in personal relationships, work, and overall quality of life, necessitating a nuanced approach to treatment that recognizes the spiritual dimensions of the disorder.

Case studies illustrate the complexities of addressing religious obsessions in therapeutic settings. One notable example involves a client who became consumed by the fear that they were blaspheming against the Holy Spirit. Despite assurances from their pastor and extensive study of religious texts affirming God's grace, the client's anxiety persisted. They engaged in compulsive prayer rituals and sought constant validation from their spiritual community. This case highlights the need for therapists to understand the interplay between mental health and spiritual beliefs, employing techniques that respect the client's faith while also addressing the underlying psychological processes.

Effective treatment strategies for religious obsessions often integrate cognitive-behavioral therapy (CBT) with spiritual counseling. CBT can help clients challenge and reframe their intrusive thoughts, while pastoral care can provide the spiritual context necessary for healing. Encouraging clients to engage in healthy religious practices without the burden of compulsive behaviors can facilitate a more balanced approach to their faith. Additionally, fostering a supportive environment where clients feel safe to express their doubts and fears can promote healing and reduce the isolation often felt by those struggling with spiritual disorders.

Ultimately, addressing religious obsessions requires a collaborative approach that includes mental health professionals and spiritual leaders working together. By recognizing the profound impact of faith on mental health, therapists and counselors can tailor their interventions to better meet the needs of individuals grappling with these challenges. This interdisciplinary approach not only aids in the therapeutic process but also promotes a deeper understanding of how faith and mental health intersect, paving the way for holistic healing that respects both psychological and spiritual dimensions.

Chapter 7: Ethical Considerations

Professional Boundaries

Professional boundaries are essential in the therapeutic and spiritual care context, serving as a framework that governs the interactions between therapists, counselors, pastors, and ministers with their clients. These boundaries are not just ethical guidelines but are crucial for maintaining a safe and effective therapeutic environment. They help prevent the blurring of roles, which can lead to conflicts of interest, feelings of betrayal, or exploitation. For professionals working with individuals experiencing spiritual disorders, clear boundaries ensure that the therapeutic process remains focused on the client's healing and growth rather than on the personal beliefs or needs of the caregiver.

Establishing professional boundaries begins with self-awareness. Therapists and spiritual leaders must recognize their own beliefs, biases, and emotional triggers that may influence their interactions with clients. This self-awareness allows professionals to approach each client with an open mind, creating a space where clients feel safe to explore their spiritual issues without feeling judged or influenced by the therapist's personal views. It is also important for professionals to engage in regular supervision or consultation to reflect on their practice and ensure that they are not inadvertently crossing boundaries that could compromise the therapeutic relationship.

Communication is a vital component of maintaining professional boundaries. Therapists and spiritual caregivers should openly discuss the nature of their relationship with clients at the outset of their work together. This includes clarifying the roles they will play, the expectations for confidentiality, and the limitations of their services. By establishing these parameters, clients can better understand the scope of the help they will receive and feel empowered to express any discomfort they may experience during the therapeutic process. This proactive approach to communication fosters trust and allows for a more transparent relationship.

In the context of spiritual disorders, the complexity of the issues faced by clients can challenge established boundaries. For instance, a client may seek guidance not only for mental health issues but also for profound existential questions or spiritual crises. In such cases, therapists must navigate their own spiritual beliefs while remaining neutral and supportive of the client's spiritual journey. This requires a delicate balance; professionals must provide a safe space for exploration without imposing their own beliefs, which could undermine the client's autonomy and therapeutic progress.

Finally, professionals must be vigilant in recognizing signs of boundary violations, which can manifest in various forms, such as dual relationships, inappropriate self-disclosure, or over-identification with clients. These violations can severely impact the client's healing process and may lead to further psychological distress. Continuous education on ethical standards and boundary management is essential for therapists, counselors, and spiritual leaders. By prioritizing professional boundaries, they can ensure that their practice remains a source of healing and support, guiding clients through their spiritual and mental health challenges effectively and compassionately.

Respecting Diverse Beliefs

Respecting diverse beliefs is essential in the therapeutic process, particularly when addressing spiritual disorders that may intersect with mental health issues. Mental health professionals, including therapists, counselors, and spiritual leaders, often encounter clients whose beliefs, practices, and values differ significantly from their own. Understanding and respecting these diverse perspectives is crucial for establishing a trusting therapeutic relationship, which can enhance the effectiveness of treatment. By recognizing the significance of a client's belief system, therapists can better tailor their approaches, ensuring that interventions are culturally sensitive and relevant to the individual's spiritual context.

Clients may present with spiritual disorders that reflect their unique belief systems, which can complicate diagnosis and treatment. For instance, what might be perceived as a mental health issue in one cultural context could be viewed as a spiritual crisis in another. Therapists must be aware of these nuances to avoid misdiagnosis and to provide appropriate support. This requires ongoing education and self-reflection about one's own biases and assumptions regarding spirituality and mental health. By adopting a stance of curiosity and openness, practitioners can create a safe space for clients to explore their beliefs without fear of judgment or misunderstanding.

Incorporating diverse spiritual beliefs into therapeutic practice also involves recognizing the potential for spirituality to serve as a source of strength and resilience. Many clients draw upon their faith or spiritual practices as coping mechanisms during times of distress. By acknowledging and validating these beliefs, therapists can empower clients to harness their spiritual resources as part of their healing journey. This approach not only respects the client's individuality but also aligns treatment with their values, potentially leading to more favorable outcomes in therapy.

Moreover, respecting diverse beliefs extends beyond individual therapy sessions. It encompasses the need for collaboration among mental health professionals, spiritual leaders, and community organizations. Interdisciplinary approaches can foster a more holistic understanding of client experiences and promote comprehensive care that addresses both mental health and spiritual needs. By engaging in dialogues and partnerships with various faith communities, therapists can enhance their cultural competence and gain insights into how different belief systems inform mental health practices.

Finally, creating an inclusive therapeutic environment requires ongoing commitment to education and advocacy for clients from diverse backgrounds. Mental health professionals must actively seek to understand the spiritual dimensions of their clients' lives, engaging with their beliefs in a respectful and supportive manner. By doing so, therapists not only enhance their own practice but also contribute to a more inclusive and compassionate mental health landscape. This commitment to respecting diverse beliefs is not merely an ethical obligation; it is a pivotal component of effective and empathetic care in addressing spiritual disorders within the broader context of mental health.

Navigating Conflicts of Interest

Navigating conflicts of interest in therapeutic settings is crucial for maintaining professional integrity and ensuring that clients receive the best possible care. For therapists, counselors, pastors, and ministers engaged in spiritual healing, the potential for conflicts of interest can arise in various forms, including dual relationships, personal beliefs, and financial incentives. Recognizing and addressing these conflicts is essential to uphold ethical standards and foster an environment conducive to healing and growth.

One of the primary conflicts of interest arises when therapists or spiritual leaders have dual relationships with clients. This situation can occur if a therapist also serves in a pastoral role within the same community or if personal relationships exist outside the therapeutic context. Such dual roles can compromise the objectivity of the therapist and may lead to biased judgments, affecting the therapeutic process. It is essential for professionals to establish clear boundaries and maintain a focus on the client's best interests, ensuring that their personal relationships do not interfere with the therapeutic alliance.

Another significant aspect of conflicts of interest involves the influence of personal beliefs on the therapeutic process. Therapists and spiritual leaders often bring their own spiritual and religious perspectives into their practice. While these beliefs can enhance the healing process for some clients, they may also create a bias that undermines the client's autonomy. It is vital for professionals to remain aware of their beliefs and how they may shape their interactions with clients. Engaging in regular self-reflection and supervision can help therapists recognize any potential biases, thereby allowing them to provide a more balanced and client-centered approach to healing.

Financial incentives can also pose a conflict of interest, particularly when therapists or ministers receive compensation for recommending specific spiritual practices or interventions. This scenario can create a situation where the professional's financial gain may overshadow the client's needs. To navigate *this potential conflict, professionals should prioritize transparency regarding any financial arrangements and ensure that their recommendations are based solely on the client's well-being rather than personal profit. Establishing clear policies and guidelines regarding financial matters can help mitigate these conflicts and maintain trust in the therapeutic relationship.*

Ultimately, navigating conflicts of interest requires a commitment to ethical practice and a dedication to the principles of spiritual healing. Professionals must actively engage in ongoing education about ethical standards, seek supervision when necessary, and cultivate an open dialogue with clients about any potential conflicts that may arise. By prioritizing the client's needs and maintaining professional integrity, therapists, counselors, pastors, and ministers can foster a healing environment that respects both the spiritual and psychological dimensions of their work. This approach not only enhances the therapeutic process but also upholds the sacred trust placed in these professionals by their clients.

Chapter 8: Collaborating with Spiritual Leaders

Building Partnerships

Building partnerships among therapists, counselors, pastors, and ministers is essential for addressing the complex interplay of spiritual disorders and mental health. Collaboration across these disciplines can enhance the understanding of how spiritual issues manifest as mental disorders, leading to more effective treatment strategies. By establishing a network of support that includes various perspectives, professionals can create a holistic approach to diagnosis and healing that acknowledges the spiritual dimensions of mental health.

One foundational aspect of building partnerships is the recognition of the unique expertise each discipline brings to the table. Therapists and counselors often possess a deep understanding of psychological theories and therapeutic techniques, while pastors and ministers may offer insights into spiritual practices and community support. By sharing knowledge and resources, these professionals can create a comprehensive framework for understanding spiritual disorders. This collaboration can lead to more thorough assessments and tailored interventions that address both the psychological and spiritual needs of individuals.

Effective communication is critical in fostering strong partnerships. Regular meetings and discussions can facilitate the sharing of case studies, insights, and treatment outcomes among professionals from different backgrounds. Creating a common language to discuss spiritual disorders can help bridge the gap between secular and faith-based approaches. This dialogue allows for the identification of overlapping concerns, enabling professionals to work together more effectively and to provide clients with a more cohesive healing experience.

Training and workshops can also play a significant role in building partnerships. By hosting joint training sessions, therapists, counselors, pastors, and ministers can learn from one another and develop a shared understanding of how *spiritual disorders impact mental health. These educational opportunities can enhance skills in recognizing symptoms, understanding the nuances of spiritual distress, and employing appropriate interventions. As professionals gain insights into each other's methodologies, they can develop a collaborative approach that respects both psychological and spiritual aspects of healing.*

Finally, establishing referral systems can strengthen partnerships and improve client care. When therapists and counselors recognize the need for spiritual guidance, they can refer clients to pastors and ministers who are equipped to address those specific issues. Conversely, spiritual leaders can refer individuals experiencing mental health challenges to qualified therapists. This reciprocal relationship not only ensures that clients receive comprehensive care, but also fosters a sense of community among professionals dedicated to promoting well-being. By building these partnerships, therapists, counselors, pastors, and ministers can work together to address the complexities of spiritual disorders, ultimately leading to more effective and meaningful healing for clients.

Referral Processes

Referral processes are essential in the context of addressing spiritual disorders that may impact mental health. Therapists, counselors, pastors, and ministers must establish clear pathways for referral to ensure that individuals receive the comprehensive care they need. This involves understanding the nature of spiritual disorders and recognizing when a client may benefit from additional support beyond spiritual guidance or therapeutic intervention. A well-defined referral process allows professionals to collaborate effectively, ensuring that clients are guided toward appropriate resources and specialists who can address their specific needs.

The first step in an effective referral process is the assessment of the client's condition. Therapists and counselors should be equipped with tools to identify spiritual disorders as classified in the Diagnostic and Statistical Manual of Spiritual Disorders. By recognizing symptoms and understanding their potential impact on mental health, professionals can determine whether a referral is necessary. This assessment should not only focus on the spiritual dimension but also consider the client's emotional, psychological, and social contexts. The goal is to create a holistic understanding of the client's issues, which will inform the referral decision.

Once a referral is deemed appropriate, professionals must communicate effectively with the client about the decision. It is crucial to explain the rationale behind the referral, emphasizing how it can benefit their overall healing journey. Transparency in discussing the referral process helps clients feel supported and understood, reducing any potential anxiety they may have regarding external interventions. Providing reassurance and outlining what to expect can empower clients to engage positively with the referral process, fostering a sense of partnership in their healing.

Collaboration among various professionals is vital for a successful referral process. Therapists, counselors, and spiritual leaders should establish networks with mental health professionals, spiritual directors, and other relevant specialists. Building these relationships enables seamless communication and coordination of care. When professionals work together, they can share insights and strategies that enhance the client's experience and outcomes. Understanding each other's roles and expertise also allows for a more integrated approach to treatment, which is particularly important for individuals experiencing complex spiritual and mental health issues.

Finally, monitoring and follow-up are critical components of the referral process. After a client has been referred, the referring professional should stay engaged, checking in on the client's progress and ensuring that they are receiving the necessary support from the referred specialist. This ongoing relationship reinforces a sense of care and commitment to the client's well-being. Additionally, feedback from the specialist can inform future sessions and interventions, creating a feedback loop that enhances the overall therapeutic process. By prioritizing these steps, professionals can ensure that referral processes are effective, compassionate, and aligned with the client's journey toward healing.

Joint Interventions

Joint interventions represent a collaborative approach to addressing spiritual disorders that manifest as mental health issues. In the context of therapeutic practice, these interventions involve the integration of various disciplines, including psychology, pastoral care, and community support. By combining the insights and techniques from these fields, practitioners can create a more holistic treatment plan that acknowledges the complex interplay between spiritual beliefs and mental well-being. This synergy can enhance the therapeutic process, fostering a deeper understanding of the patient's experiences and promoting more effective healing.

One of the key components of joint interventions is the establishment of a multidisciplinary team. This team may include therapists, counselors, spiritual leaders, and other healthcare professionals who work together to assess and address the needs of the individual. Each member brings unique expertise to the table, allowing for a comprehensive evaluation that considers both spiritual and psychological dimensions. This collaborative effort can lead to more accurate diagnoses and tailored treatment plans that respect the individual's faith and spiritual practices while addressing their mental health concerns.

Effective communication is crucial in joint interventions. Team members must engage in open dialogue to share insights and observations about the individual's condition. This communication ensures that all aspects of the person's life are taken into account, from their spiritual beliefs to their psychological symptoms. Regular meetings and case discussions can facilitate this exchange of ideas, fostering a cohesive approach to treatment. Furthermore, involving the individual in these discussions, when appropriate, can empower them and enhance their commitment to the healing process.

Incorporating spiritual practices into therapeutic interventions can also play a significant role in joint approaches. Techniques such as prayer, meditation, and spiritual counseling can complement traditional therapeutic methods, offering individuals a sense of hope and connection. These practices can provide comfort and strength, helping individuals navigate their *mental health challenges while remaining anchored in their faith. Therapists and spiritual leaders should work together to identify which practices resonate with the individual and how they can be safely integrated into the treatment plan.*

Ultimately, joint interventions highlight the importance of a comprehensive approach to healing that respects the individual's spiritual journey. By fostering collaboration among various disciplines, practitioners can address the multifaceted nature of spiritual disorders that affect mental health. This integrative strategy not only enriches the therapeutic experience but also promotes a deeper understanding of how faith and spirituality can be powerful allies in the healing process. Through this synergy, therapists, counselors, and spiritual leaders can work together to guide individuals toward recovery, emphasizing the importance of both psychological support and spiritual nourishment.

Chapter 9: Future Directions in Therapy

Emerging Research

Emerging research in the field of faith and healing is uncovering significant insights into the relationship between spirituality and mental health. Recent studies demonstrate that spiritual practices can positively influence psychological well-being, providing a complementary approach to traditional therapeutic techniques. These findings are particularly relevant for therapists, counselors, and spiritual leaders who seek to understand the intricate dynamics between spiritual disorders and mental health issues. By integrating spiritual assessments into clinical practice, professionals can better address the holistic needs of their clients.

One area of focus in emerging research is the role of prayer and meditation in alleviating symptoms of mental disorders. Studies have indicated that individuals who engage in regular prayer or mindfulness meditation report lower levels of anxiety and depression. This suggests that incorporating spiritual practices into therapeutic settings can enhance the efficacy of treatment plans. Therapists are encouraged to explore these modalities with their clients, fostering an environment where spiritual expression is valued and integrated into the healing process.

Another significant aspect of emerging research involves the identification and classification of spiritual disorders, as outlined in the Diagnostic and Statistical Manual of Spiritual Disorders. This framework aims to provide clinicians with a robust understanding of how spiritual crises can manifest as mental health challenges. As therapists become more familiar with this classification, they can better discern when a client's struggles may be rooted in spiritual disconnection rather than purely psychological disorders. This distinction is crucial for developing appropriate intervention strategies that address the underlying spiritual issues.

Furthermore, research is increasingly highlighting the importance of community and social support in the healing process. Faith-based communities often provide a network of support that can be invaluable for individuals facing mental health challenges. Emerging studies suggest that clients who actively engage with their spiritual communities experience enhanced resilience and a greater sense of belonging, which can mitigate feelings of isolation often associated with mental disorders. Therapists and counselors are encouraged to consider the role of community in their treatment approaches, facilitating connections between clients and supportive spiritual networks.

Lastly, the intersection of cultural spirituality and mental health is gaining attention in emerging research. Different cultural backgrounds bring diverse spiritual beliefs and practices that can impact the therapeutic process. Understanding these cultural nuances is essential for therapists working with clients from various backgrounds. Incorporating culturally relevant spiritual practices into therapy not only validates the client's experiences but also enhances the therapeutic alliance. As emerging research continues to unfold, it is vital for mental health professionals to stay informed about these developments, ensuring they provide culturally competent care that respects and honors the spiritual dimensions of their clients' lives.

Integrating Spirituality in Clinical Practice

Integrating spirituality into clinical practice involves recognizing the profound impact that spiritual beliefs and practices can have on a client's mental health. As therapists, counselors, pastors, and ministers, it is essential to understand the interplay between spirituality and mental health, particularly when addressing spiritual disorders as outlined in the Diagnostic and Statistical Manual of Spiritual Disorders. This integration requires a nuanced approach that respects the client's spiritual beliefs while also addressing any mental health challenges they may face.

One of the first steps in integrating spirituality into clinical practice is to create a safe and open environment where clients feel comfortable discussing their spiritual beliefs. This can be achieved by asking open-ended questions about their spiritual experiences and beliefs during initial assessments. Understanding a client's spiritual background can provide valuable insights into their coping mechanisms, values, and sources of support. Practitioners should remain nonjudgmental and curious, allowing clients to express their spirituality in their own terms, which can enhance the therapeutic alliance.

Moreover, practitioners can incorporate spiritual assessments into their evaluations to identify potential spiritual disorders that may be contributing to a client's mental health issues. Tools such as the Spiritual Assessment Inventory or the HOPE model can facilitate this process. By assessing spiritual well-being, practitioners can better understand how spiritual distress may manifest in symptoms such as anxiety, depression, or existential crises. This understanding can guide the development of tailored treatment plans that address both spiritual and psychological needs.

Therapeutic interventions can also include the integration of spiritual practices such as mindfulness, meditation, prayer, or rituals that resonate with the client's beliefs. These practices can serve as effective coping strategies that promote healing and resilience. For instance, mindfulness meditation can help clients cultivate awareness and acceptance, reducing symptoms of anxiety and depression. It is crucial for practitioners to be knowledgeable about various spiritual practices and to collaborate with clients in selecting those that align with their values and preferences.

Finally, ongoing education and reflection on one's own spiritual beliefs are vital for practitioners in this field. Understanding personal biases and how they may influence clinical work can help in providing more effective and empathetic care. Engaging in supervision or peer discussions about spirituality in therapy can provide valuable insights and support. By fostering a continual learning environment, therapists can enhance their ability to integrate spirituality into clinical practice, ultimately benefiting their clients as they navigate the complexities of mental health and spiritual well-being.

Advocacy for Spiritual Wellness

Advocacy for spiritual wellness involves recognizing the integral role spirituality plays in overall mental health. Therapists, counselors, pastors, and ministers must understand that spiritual disorders can significantly impact an individual's mental state, influencing their emotional well-being and coping mechanisms. The Diagnostic and Statistical Manual of Spiritual Disorders serves as a vital resource for identifying and addressing these issues. By advocating for spiritual wellness, professionals can facilitate healing processes that encompass both mental and spiritual dimensions, leading to more effective therapeutic outcomes.

A key aspect of advocacy for spiritual wellness is the incorporation of spiritual assessments in therapeutic practices.

This involves evaluating clients' spiritual beliefs, practices, and experiences as part of their overall mental health assessment. By doing so, practitioners can gain deeper insights into the factors contributing to their clients' spiritual disorders. This holistic approach enables therapists to tailor their interventions more effectively, supporting clients in finding meaning, purpose, and connection through their spiritual lives. Additionally, understanding spiritual beliefs can help in identifying potential sources of distress, allowing for a more comprehensive treatment plan.

Collaboration between mental health professionals and spiritual leaders is essential in promoting spiritual wellness. By forming partnerships, therapists and ministers can create a supportive network that addresses the multifaceted needs of individuals experiencing spiritual disorders. This collaboration can lead to the development of community programs that incorporate spiritual practices, such as meditation, prayer, and mindfulness, into therapeutic settings. Such initiatives can foster a sense of belonging and support, enhancing the healing journey for individuals grappling with mental health challenges tied to spiritual issues.

Education plays a crucial role in advocating for spiritual wellness. Therapists and counselors should engage in ongoing training regarding the intersection of spirituality and mental health. This education can equip them with the skills necessary to recognize spiritual disorders and address them effectively within their therapeutic practices. Furthermore, raising awareness about the significance of spirituality in mental health can help reduce stigma associated with spiritual struggles, encouraging individuals to seek help without fear of judgment. Empowering professionals through education ultimately leads to better care for clients.

Finally, advocating for spiritual wellness means promoting self-care for both practitioners and their clients. Mental health professionals often bear the emotional weight of their clients' struggles, making it imperative for them to cultivate their spiritual wellness as well. By engaging in their spiritual practices and reflecting on their beliefs, therapists can enhance their resilience and effectiveness in their roles. Encouraging clients to explore their spiritual dimensions can also serve as a powerful tool for recovery. This dual focus on self-care and client care fosters a more compassionate and empathetic therapeutic environment, ultimately benefiting all involved.

Chapter 10: Resources for Practitioners

Recommended Readings

For professionals seeking to deepen their understanding of the intersection between spirituality and mental health, a range of literature provides valuable insights and frameworks. One essential text is "The Spiritual Competency Resource Kit" by Dr. Pamela A. Hays, which offers practical guidance for integrating spiritual considerations into therapeutic practice. This resource is especially beneficial for therapists and counselors looking to navigate spiritual issues sensitively and effectively, ensuring that they address the holistic needs of their clients while remaining mindful of the potential for spiritual disorders as outlined in the Diagnostic and Statistical Manual of Spiritual Disorders.

Another pivotal reading is "Healing the Soul: Psychoanalytic Healers and the Spiritual Life" by Dr. Robert A. Neimeyer. This book explores the therapeutic journey through a spiritual lens, highlighting how different therapeutic modalities can incorporate spiritual healing. It is a comprehensive examination of how psychotherapy can benefit from spiritual wisdom, making it a valuable resource for ministers and pastoral counselors aiming to support individuals facing spiritual crises. Neimeyer's work underscores the importance of recognizing and validating the spiritual dimensions of clients' experiences.

"Spiritually Integrated Psychotherapy: An Empirical Guide to Concepts, Methods, and Practice" by Dr. Mark R. McMinn and Dr. Timothy R. Phillips provides a systematic approach to understanding how spiritual integration can enhance therapeutic outcomes. This book is particularly useful for therapists who wish to incorporate spiritual elements into their practice without compromising the integrity of psychological principles. McMinn and Phillips present empirical evidence supporting the efficacy of spiritually integrated approaches, making it an essential addition to any professional's library.

For those interested in a more research-oriented perspective, "The Handbook of Religion and Health" edited by Harold G. Koenig is indispensable. This comprehensive volume compiles studies examining the impact of religious beliefs and practices on mental health. It provides therapists and counselors with evidence-based insights into how spirituality can influence psychological well-being, offering a critical resource for understanding the broader implications of spiritual disorders. The findings presented in this handbook can inform clinical practice and enhance the ability to address spiritual concerns within therapeutic settings.

Finally, "Spirituality and Mental Health: A Handbook for the Helping Professions" by Dr. Steven J. Sandage and Dr. Kenneth I. Pargament is a significant contribution to the field. This book synthesizes current research on spirituality and mental health, providing practical strategies for integrating spirituality into therapeutic practice. It is particularly relevant for pastors and ministers who often encounter spiritual dilemmas in their work. Sandage and Pargament emphasize the importance of addressing spiritual distress and offer frameworks for understanding the role of spirituality in healing, making it a vital resource for those involved in spiritual care and counseling.

Professional Organizations

Professional organizations play a crucial role in the field of therapy and counseling, particularly when it comes to addressing the intersection of spiritual disorders and mental health. These organizations provide valuable resources, training, and support for therapists, counselors, pastors, and ministers who are navigating the complexities of spiritual issues that may contribute to mental disorders. By engaging with these professional bodies, practitioners can enhance their understanding of the Diagnostic and Statistical Manual of Spiritual Disorders, which aims to bridge the gap between spiritual beliefs and mental health treatments.

One of the primary benefits of joining professional organizations is access to up-to-date research and best practices related to the treatment of spiritual disorders. Many organizations publish journals, conduct conferences, and offer workshops that focus on the latest findings in the field. This ongoing education is vital for therapists and counselors, as it allows them to remain informed about emerging trends and evidence-based interventions. Such knowledge empowers professionals to provide comprehensive care that respects clients' spiritual beliefs while effectively addressing their mental health needs.

Networking opportunities within professional organizations also foster collaboration and support among practitioners. Members can connect with like-minded professionals who share similar interests and challenges in integrating spiritual care into therapeutic practices. This exchange of ideas can lead to the development of innovative approaches and interventions that are sensitive to the spiritual dimensions of mental health. Additionally, mentorship programs often available through these organizations can help newer practitioners gain insights from experienced colleagues, further enriching their professional growth.

Ethical guidelines provided by professional organizations are essential for ensuring that therapists and counselors navigate the delicate balance between spirituality and mental health care responsibly. These guidelines help practitioners understand the boundaries of their roles when addressing spiritual issues in therapy. They emphasize the importance of respecting clients' beliefs while providing care that is grounded in psychological principles. By adhering to these ethical standards, professionals can create a safe environment for clients to explore their spiritual concerns without fear of judgment or coercion.

Finally, professional organizations often engage in advocacy efforts that promote the recognition of spiritual disorders within the broader mental health community. By raising awareness about the impact of spiritual issues on mental well-being, these organizations work to reduce stigma and encourage more holistic approaches to mental health treatment. Through initiatives that highlight the importance of integrating spirituality into therapeutic practices, they contribute to a growing acceptance of the need for comprehensive care that addresses both mental and spiritual health. As therapists, counselors, pastors, and ministers become more involved with these organizations, they can play a vital role in shaping the future of mental health treatment that honors the spiritual dimensions of human experience.

Workshops and Training Opportunities

Workshops and training opportunities tailored for therapists, counselors, pastors, and ministers play a crucial role in bridging the gap between spiritual and mental health. These programs are designed to equip professionals with the knowledge and skills necessary to identify and address spiritual disorders that may contribute to mental health issues. By participating in workshops, practitioners can gain insights into the Diagnostic and Statistical Manual of Spiritual Disorders, which provides a framework for understanding the interplay between spiritual beliefs and mental wellbeing.

One of the primary objectives of these workshops is to enhance the understanding of spiritual disorders and their manifestations in clients. Participants learn to recognize symptoms that may be attributed to spiritual crises, such as feelings of abandonment, existential despair, or loss of faith. Through case studies and experiential exercises, attendees can develop diagnostic skills that help differentiate between purely psychological issues and those rooted in spiritual concerns, thus facilitating a more comprehensive approach to treatment.

Training opportunities also focus on integrating spiritual care into therapeutic practices. This integration is essential for providing holistic support to clients, as many individuals seek therapy not only for mental health reasons but also for spiritual guidance. Workshops often cover various modalities, such as mindfulness, prayer, and meditation, which can be incorporated into therapy sessions. By learning these techniques, practitioners can support clients in exploring their spiritual beliefs while addressing mental health challenges, ultimately fostering a more profound healing experience.

Furthermore, professional development in this area encourages collaboration among different disciplines. Workshops often bring together therapists, counselors, and spiritual leaders to share insights and strategies. This multidisciplinary approach allows participants to explore diverse perspectives on spiritual disorders, leading to a richer understanding of how faith and spirituality influence mental health. Such collaboration can also create referral networks, ensuring that clients receive comprehensive care that addresses both their psychological and spiritual needs.

In conclusion, workshops and training opportunities are vital for professionals working at the intersection of faith and mental health. They provide the tools necessary for understanding and diagnosing spiritual disorders while equipping practitioners with techniques to support their clients holistically. As the field continues to evolve, ongoing education in these areas will be essential for effectively addressing the complex relationship between spirituality and mental wellbeing, ultimately enhancing the quality of care provided to individuals in need.

FOR BOOKINGS AND SPEAKING ENGAGEMENTS

DR. SHAMEKA R CAMPBELL

drpointer.openheart@gmail.com

SOCIAL MEDIA SITES :

FACEBOOK: SHAMEKA R CAMPBELL

INSTAGRAM: OPEN HEART INTERNATIONAL

YOUTUBE: OPEN HEART INTERNATIONAL OF ATLANTA

FOR COUNSELING SERVICES : OPEN HEART COUNSELING

PSYCHOLOGY TODAY

THERAPY TRIBE